CERAMICS
FROM CLAY TO KILN

by Harvey Weiss

YOUNG SCOTT BOOKS

Table of Contents

OTHER TITLES BY THE SAME AUTHOR IN THE

Beginning Artist's Library

1. SCULPTURE: *Clay, Wood & Wire*
2. PRINTMAKING: *Paper, Ink & Roller*
3. DRAWING: *Pencil, Pen & Brush*
4. CRAFTS: *Sticks, Spools & Feathers*
5. CRAFTS: *Collage and Construction*
6. PAINTING: *Paint, Brush & Palette*

© MCMLXIV BY HARVEY WEISS
PRINTED IN THE U.S.A.
LIBRARY OF CONGRESS CATALOG CARD NO. 64-13583
SBN: 201-09153-4
ALL RIGHTS RESERVED
YOUNG SCOTT BOOKS
A DIVISION OF ADDISON-WESLEY PUBLISHING COMPANY, INC.
READING, MASSACHUSETTS 01867

SONG OF THE VOWELS,
by Jacques Lipchitz

*Museum of Modern Art
New York*

Introduction

If you take a lump of clay, shape it, and put it into a hot fire, it will become a hard, permanent object. This process is called ceramics.

It is an exciting process, because you start with a raw and formless and common material and make it into something graceful and useful—a bowl, an ashtray, a birdhouse, a statue. This making of something elegant and useful from a lump of humble clay—making something out of nothing — is a challenging and satisfying experience.

There are a few basic things you *must* learn before you start to work with clay. Read the following four pages carefully. They contain the ABC's of ceramics.

Materials, Methods and Tools

Where To Get Clay

The simplest way to get clay is to buy it from an art or ceramics supply store. But it is possible that you live in a section of the country where there are some good natural clay formations. Then you can dig into the side of a cliff, or bed of a stream, or a few feet into the ground, and—if you're lucky—you'll find all the clay you could ever use. Ask some people who know the neighboring countryside. They may know if there is clay anywhere around, and where to find it.

If you buy your clay—and you probably will—try to get terra cotta clay with "grog." Grog is burnt clay that has been ground up and mixed with the natural clay. Its purpose is to minimize the danger of splitting and cracking of the finished piece during the firing. You can, of course, use clay without grog. Terra cotta clay has a handsome reddish color when wet. It is a rich pink after firing.

There are many kinds of clays, varying in color and feel. The one kind to avoid is plasticene, which is not really clay, but an oil-base material not intended for firing.

Clay is sometimes sold in powder form. If this is the only kind you can get, you'll have to mix it with water. Powder clay is usually sold packed in a plastic bag. In this case you simply pour a little water into the bag and mix by kneading the bag.

The Firing Of Clay

If clay is left to stand for two or three days the water in it will evaporate. The clay will dry out and become rather brittle and fragile. If handled or moved about it will eventually fall apart. But it will return to its original plastic state if you add water to it. In order for clay to become a strong and permanent material it must be baked in a very hot furnace—to approximately 2,000 degrees Fahrenheit. This process is called firing, and the furnace is called a kiln. Once clay has been fired, it will not be softened by water.

The cheapest kiln you can buy costs about forty dollars. The chances are you won't acquire one of your own until you've had a good deal of experience with ceramics. But there is usually some place where you can take your clay pieces to be fired. Most schools have a kiln. Many ceramic supply stores have firing facilities, or will be able to tell you of someone who has a kiln and will fire your work for a small charge. Perhaps you know somebody who has a small kiln and will let you use it. More details on firing, glazes, and such technical matters can be found at the end of this book.

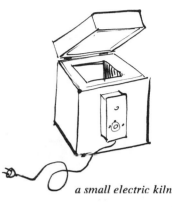

a small electric kiln

How To Prepare Clay For Use

If a piece of clay has air bubbles or air pockets inside it and is put into a kiln, the trapped air will expand in the enormous heat and cause the clay to shatter. The clay will actually explode! Therefore it is important that all air be eliminated from the clay before you use it. The process of removing the air from clay and getting it into a workable condition is called "wedging."

You wedge clay by taking a lump about as big as your two fists and cutting it in half with a thin wire. Then the two halves are either slammed vigorously together, or slammed down hard on a table top. Do this twenty or thirty times until the clay is an even consistency and free from lumps and air bubbles. You can tell when the clay is properly wedged by cutting a piece in half and looking to see if any air bubbles show on the cut surface. If there are still bubbles, wedge some more. Never use clay that hasn't been wedged.

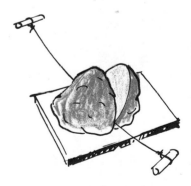

cutting with wire

Clay is a responsive material, but it won't handle well unless it is the right consistency. If it is too soft and mushy, it will feel like mud, and you won't be able to control it. If, on the other hand, it is stiff and hard, it will be difficult to manipulate. Clay that is too wet should be spread out flat on a rag and allowed to dry out for an hour or two. If the clay is too dry, pour some water over it and knead it until you are satisfied with its feel and can shape it easily.

How To Care For Clay

Unless clay is kept damp it will dry out. Store it in a plastic bucket with a lid, or any waterproof container that can be tightly closed. Keep a wet rag on top of the clay, and take a look at it every so often to make sure it is not drying out. If it seems to be getting stiff and hard, pour a little water on the rag.

When a piece you are working on is left for any length of time, such as overnight, you must see that it doesn't dry out. Wrap it with thin plastic sheeting. This will keep all the moisture in, and keep the clay in a workable state for a long time.

The Drying Of Clay

Clay must be completely dry before it can be fired. And when it dries, it shrinks in size. The shrinkage amounts to 10 or 15 per cent depending on the kind of clay. This is a great deal. If one part of a clay piece shrinks faster than an adjoining part it will pull apart. You will get splits and cracks, and the entire piece may be ruined.

So it is essential for clay to dry out evenly. If you make a simple tile, or square of clay, it will dry evenly all over because there are no thin parts or projections. But if you made a bowl like the one illustrated in the margin, the handle would dry out much faster than the rest of the bowl, and would probably crack off. In order to avoid this, put a small damp rag around the area that would dry out first.

After a clay piece has dried for approximately twenty-four hours, it will become fairly rigid, but it can still be worked on. In this state it is called "leather hard." It can be handled without fear of getting it out of shape, and imperfections can be removed by scraping or rubbing, or the surface can be decorated by scratching or carving with a sharp tool.

Joining Clay

When you want to join separate pieces of clay, you must use a mushy clay mixture called "slip." It works like glue. Slip is made by taking some clay and adding water until you get a very soft, cream-like consistency. To join the pieces, first roughen the two areas that are to be joined. This is done by scratching with a pointed tool. Then, with a brush or stick, smear on a liberal coating of slip. Firmly press the two pieces together.

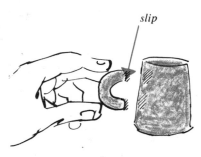

slip

Tools Needed For Working In Clay

For wedging your clay you'll need a thin piece of wire about 18 inches long. The wire will be easier to handle if you wrap the ends around two short pieces of wood.

You can buy a wood modeling stick like the one illustrated, or you can whittle one yourself. It is a useful tool, especially if it has a little wire loop at one end. This is used for gouging out clay.

A sharp knife is necessary for cutting the clay, and a popsicle stick or tongue depressor, some rags, a ruler, and a few small blocks of wood will also come in handy.

For rolling out flat slabs of clay you'll want a large cylindrical object, such as a rolling pin or a piece of pipe, two strips of wood ½ inch thick and 18 inches long, and some thin nails. You'll also need a few pieces of board upon which to place your work. A good, strong work table, spread with newspapers, and in a good light, is essential.

The best tools of all you won't have to go far to find. They are your fingers. Other tools are really extensions of these ten essential tools.

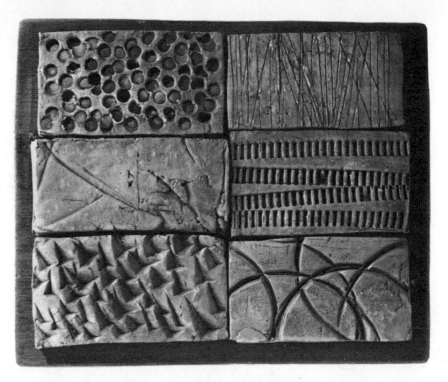

Getting Started with Clay

What can you do with clay? What are its possibilities? The best way to find out is by doing a little experimenting. The sort of small tiles illustrated on the opposite page are ideal for this purpose.

Making these tiles can teach you a great deal, and they can also be put to some practical use. They can be hung on a wall, or set into cement, or used as paper weights. A group of four or six tiles can be glued to a board and used as a trivet.

To make tiles like these you will need a board about 8 by 18 inches, a rag, two strips of wood ½ inch thick and 18 inches long, some thin nails, and a rolling pin or a piece of pipe.

How To Make Tiles

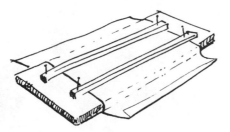

1. Spread the rag over the board. (The purpose of the rag is to keep the clay from sticking to the board.) Lightly nail the two strips of wood over the rag.

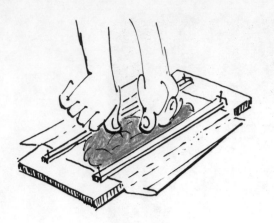

2. Take a lump of clay out of your clay bucket. A piece about the size of a large apple will do. Wedge it thoroughly, as described on pages 5 and 6. Spread the wedged clay between the two strips of wood.

3. Go back and forth over the clay with your rolling pin, until the clay is completely flat and even.

4. Now pry up the wood strips. With a knife cut the clay into neat rectangular pieces about 2 by 3½ inches.

These are your basic, unadorned tiles. Now see what you can do with them. What will the clay *permit* you to do with them? Try scratching lines with a knife. See if you can develop some kind of nice looking pattern. Take another tile and poke it with the point of a pencil—with the eraser end—with the side. Press into another tile with the corner of a scrap of wood, or a paper clip, or comb, or spoon, or whatever else you can find. These varied surfaces you can give to clay are called "textures." They are an important element in the design of ceramics. (The textures on page 8, reading from left to right and top to bottom, were made with a pencil point, a knife, a small block of wood, a piece of burlap, the side of a pencil, a comb, the edge of a gear wheel, a pair of pliers, the corner of a block of wood.)

Your first few tiles may get messed up from your experiments, so just throw them back into the clay bucket. Take some fresh clay, wedge it up, and roll out some more tiles. Now you'll find yourself being more confident and adventurous, and the tiles will show it. Put aside the ones you find most interesting. Let them dry for two or three days.

> NOTE: Unless you've already had a great deal of experience working with ceramics, take your time and make the various kinds of tiles described in this section before you attempt any of the other projects described further on in this book. The basic methods of ceramics are explained here, and an understanding of them is essential before you can go on to some of the more complicated projects.

Twisting and Bending

Roll out some new tiles and try bending one. You will find that you can bend a slab of clay just so far and then it will begin to crack. To prevent clay from cracking while you are working it, keep squeezing and smoothing the outside of the curve as you bend it. Take another tile and twist it. See how far you can go before it begins to crack.

Adding

Cut out some more small tiles and try joining them together with the aid of slip. Be sure to roughen both surfaces that are to be joined. Use the slip liberally. (Page 7 has instructions for the mixing and use of slip.) You might try to make a little house, or a simple geometric construction. The illustrations below will give you a few ideas of the possibilities.

When your tiles are completely dry, they can be fired. If you have the use of a kiln and are going to do the firing yourself, be sure to read the instructions on firing on page 60.

A Trivet

If you want to use some of the flat tiles you've made and fired for a trivet, get a piece of good wood such as walnut or birch or mahogany. Cut it to a size just slightly larger than the group of tiles. Bevel the edges of the wood with a file. Sandpaper carefully until the wood is smooth and clean. Then attach the tiles to the wood with a strong glue such as Duco cement, or a white casein glue such as Elmer's Glue-All, or an epoxy cement. You can use this same method for mounting the tiles for a wall plaque.

STUDY FOR THE RAPE OF LUCRECE, *by Reuben Nakian. 9¼" high, 16" long, 4¼" thick. Museum of Modern Art. This is basically a large tile, on which an abstract design has been drawn and carved. The vigorous slashes and gouges, which at first glance may seem accidental, are the lines and rhythms and movements the sculptor was interested in. He has, in fact, used the slab of clay as a painter might use a sketch pad.*

THE CITY, *by Peter Grippe. Museum of Modern Art. This is a more complex use of slabs. Many separate parts are joined to make one rather elaborate composition. Elements such as hands, noses, eyes, and lips have been added on and many lines incised.*

Clay Slabs And How To Use Them

The kind of clay slabs used in making tiles can also be used to build ashtrays, boxes and the more elaborate constructions shown on the opposite page. This way of working is almost like carpentry. But instead of wood you use slabs of clay, and instead of nails you use slip to hold the parts together.

How To Make An Ashtray

You'll need the same materials used to make the tiles described in the previous section: a board about 8 by 18 inches, two strips of wood ½ inch thick and 18 inches long, a rag, knife, ruler, rolling pin and modeling tool.

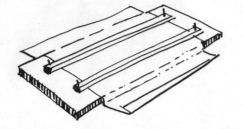

1. Spread the rag over your board and lightly nail down the two strips of wood.

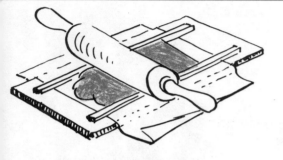

2. Wedge up a lump of clay and press it down firmly between the two strips on your board. Flatten the clay by going back and forth over it with your rolling pin.

3. Remove one of the wood strips and cut out a slab of clay for the base of your ashtray. It can be a square shape, or rectangular; about 3 by 5 inches is a good size.

4. Cut out the strips for the walls of the ashtray. Use a ruler to guide your knife. They can be tall, or short and stubby—whatever you think will look best—but all four walls must be the same height. Make the walls a little longer than needed. You'll trim them later.

5. Scratch the bottom of the first wall and the part of the base upon which it will rest. Apply a generous amount of slip to both. Then press the wall in place.

6. Repeat this for the next three walls. Be sure to scratch and use slip on the corner joints as well as at the bottom of the walls.

7. With a sharp knife cut off the protruding ends of the walls. Then cut off any excess clay from the base.

8. Make a thin roll of soft clay and use this to strengthen the inside joints and to reinforce the corners.

9. Now go over your ashtray to remove any bumps, irregularities or trickles of slip. If the walls are wavy and out of shape, tap them back into position with a little block of wood. If the clay seems a little too soft to control comfortably, set the ashtray aside for an hour or two to dry out a little.

10. If you want to add any decoration this is the time to do it. Some of the surface textures you used on the tiles might look well on your ashtray.

When you are finished, let the ashtray dry completely. (Two or three days.) Then fire it.

Compare the two ashtrays above. They are almost identical—both neatly made, equally practical and of the same size. But which do you prefer?

I would choose the one on the right. The very slight angle of the sides, the way the bottom edges are gently rounded off and the simple decorative line make this ashtray more attractive.

When you finish off your own ashtray, keep all this in mind. Try to make it handsome as well as useful.

Once you've learned how to make an ashtray, you can try more ambitious projects of this type. For example, the box on the left is built up in the same way as the ashtray.

CHEST, *Cypriote. This piece is about three thousand years old. Metropolitan Museum of Art*

The bird feeder shown on page 14 is a similar type of construction. The difference is in proportions and in that a window has been cut in the side so the birds can reach in for their food. Holes are poked through the bottom edge and near the top for wooden dowels to be inserted. The lower two are for the birds to stand on while feeding. The roof is removable, so that you can put food inside. It is assembled as shown. The bird feeder is hung from a branch of a tree by two strings.

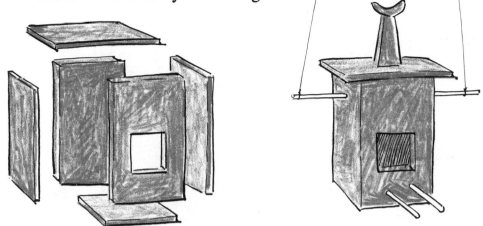

Can you think of anything else that you could build using clay slabs? What about a bird house, a little easel to display a foreign coin or medal, book ends, a candy box—?

A box with a lid can be used for cigarettes or jewelry. The handle of the lid will give you a fine chance for a little imaginative design. A few suggestions for handles are illustrated, but see if you can't think up something of your own.

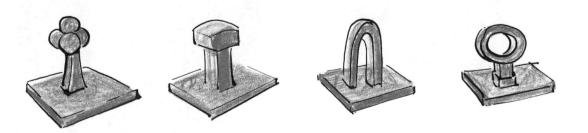

FAIENCE BOWL, *Egyptian, XVIII Dynasty*
(1580-1480 B.C.)
Metropolitan Museum of Art

20

TRIPOD BOWL, *Vera Cruz, Mexico*
American Museum of Natural History

Bowls And Pots

The ashtrays and boxes described in the preceding section use straight, flat slabs of clay. But clay slabs can, of course, be bent into a curve. The bowl illustrated at the top of this page is made of two slabs, slightly curved and then joined together.

What happens if you bend a slab all the way around into a circle? Then you have the wall of a vase or bowl. The objects illustrated on the opposite page can all be made this way.

A sugar bowl, like the one shown at the lower left is a good project for a first try at this way of working. This is how it's made:

How To Make A Sugar Bowl

1. Wedge up a lump of clay and roll it out in the same way you did for your tiles and ashtray.

2. Cut out a slab for the base of the bowl. Make it larger than needed. The excess will be trimmed off later.

3. Cut out a strip of clay for the walls of the bowl. This should be about twelve inches long, two inches high and ½ inch thick.

4. Now get a small, round glass jar, or small drinking glass. It should have straight sides with no projections. This is going to serve as a core around which the clay wall will be wrapped. Place the glass on the center of your base slab.

5. Roughen the clay base around the edge of the glass and add slip. Do the same with the bottom edge of the wall slab.

6. Wrap the wall slab around the jar, or drinking glass, and press it firmly down onto the base.

7. The wall will be a little too long, so cut off the excess and squeeze the edges together, using slip. If necessary add some soft clay and smooth neatly. This has to be done carefully or your bowl will have a bumpy, ragged seam.

8. Remove the jar. It has served its purpose now. If it doesn't come out easily, pour a little water around the edges. Then rotate it slowly, gradually twisting it out. If it still doesn't come out, lift it up, clay and all, and poke a little hole through the clay on the bottom to let air in. After you have removed the jar, fill the hole with a little clay.

9. With your knife, trim off the excess clay from the base. On the inside, strengthen the seam where the wall meets the base by pressing in a thin roll of soft clay. Then smooth the outside of the seam with a flat stick.

Now you have your bowl in its rough shape. It probably looks rather crude at this point. But the clay is still soft, and you can now proceed to modify the shape. Do you want the top to flare out a bit? Would you like a little bulge in the center? Perhaps you want to make the top oval or rectangular. These are the slight variations that will give your bowl a little grace and distinction. Now is the time to "bring it to life."

Developing the Shape

In order to modify the rough shape of the bowl you will have to push out from the inside, slowly and carefully. (If you want to narrow the shape, push *in*.) Use a spoon or your fingers to push with, and always support the other side of the wall as you do this. Keep turning the bowl as you work, using very light pressure. The changes must be made *gradually*.

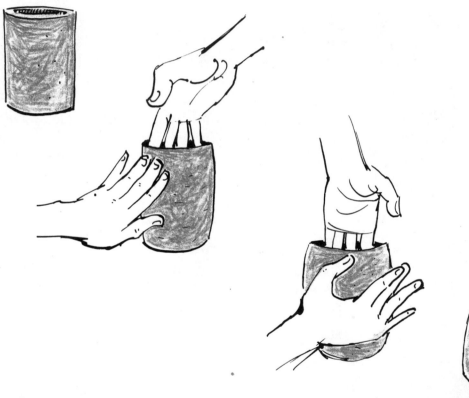

You may have a lot of trouble keeping the walls from wagging and waving. If they get too misshapen, just throw the clay back into the clay barrel and start again. That's one of the nice things about clay—you can make any number of false starts or clumsy beginnings, but you never waste material. As long as the clay isn't fired you can use it over and over again.

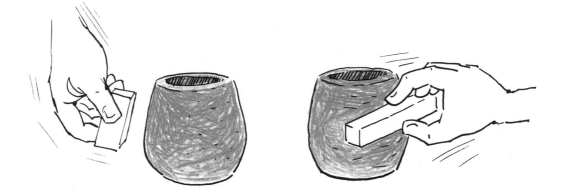

Finishing the Surface

When you are satisfied with the shape of your bowl, let it dry for two or three hours. Then work on the *surface* of the clay. Remove as many bumps and lumps as you can. A small block of wood will be useful now. Hold your fingers inside the bowl, and gently pat it with the block of wood to get the clay even and symmetrical. If you have a longer piece of wood, use a rocking motion. Don't try to get the clay as smooth and even as glass. This is almost impossible unless you have a potter's wheel. The marks that your tools leave on the surface of the clay make an interesting texture.

If you want a handle for the bowl, make it separately and attach it with slip. The drawings suggest a few possibilities. (There is really no practical reason for having a handle on a sugar bowl, but if it makes the bowl look a little nicer, that's reason enough. You might, in fact, try four or five handles on the bowl!)

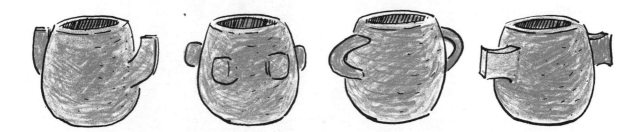

The lid of your bowl (if you want a lid) can be made as shown below. Two circular shapes and a knob will do the trick. Give some thought to the knob. This is a center of interest and an opportunity to use a little ingenuity. Finally, let the bowl dry completely. Then fire it.

A Birdhouse

There are any number of different things you can make using this curved slab method of construction. Large vases and bowls are possible. A birdhouse like the one illustrated below is basically no more than a large, upside-down version of the sugar bowl. The top has been closed in, and a little door cut into the side.

The size of the bird house and its door will determine the sort of bird that will make it a home. Hang it in a tree, well off the ground, so that no marauding cats can reach it.

A candle holder makes a nice table decoration. You could also make a holder like this with various open designs cut out of the walls — in the way that you would make a jack-o-lantern.

After you've made one or two bowls, try making one without using the glass jar as a core. Without the jar you will have a little more freedom of shape and size. You could have the walls leaning in or out, for example. And you can try making a taller bowl, using one slab of clay for the bottom section of the wall, and then adding another section of wall.

As you become familiar with this way of working, you'll find that it is not much more difficult to make a large, complex construction than a small, simple one. The only difference is the added time and patience required to make the more numerous component parts.

You'll have to pay more attention to the consistency of your clay when you build these more complicated forms. If the clay is too soft it will not support any weight on top of it, and you may have to let one section dry out for a few hours, or overnight, before adding additional sections.

PITCHER, *American Indian, New Mexico*
American Museum of Natural History

BOWL, *Chinese, 2000 B.C.*
Metropolitan Museum of Art

PITCHER, *American Indian, New Mexico*
American Museum of Natural History

Using Clay Coils

There is another way of building up hollow shapes. It is called the coil method, and it is simply the piling up of long thin "snakes" of clay—one on top of another. This way of working is a little slower than the slab method described in the previous section. But you will find that it is easier to get a variety of shapes this way. The illustrations above and on the opposite page are a few examples of this technique. Note how the bowls bulge out into full, rounded shapes. Forms like these would be quite difficult to get with clay slabs.

The coil method is one of the oldest ceramic techniques. It has been used by many primitive civilizations, as well as by modern potters. The bowl at the top of this page was made many hundreds of years ago by some Egyptian potter. The undecorated pitcher on the opposite page was made long ago by an American Indian. The thin lines show where one coil of clay was placed on top of another.

29

How To Make A Bowl From Coils

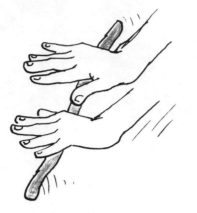

1. Wedge up some clay. Then take a lump and roll it into a "snake." Place the clay on a flat surface and lightly roll it back and forth, using a firm but gentle pressure. It should be approximately 14 inches long and as thick as your middle finger. Be sure the coil is the same thickness throughout its length. Make ten or twelve coils, and cover them with a damp rag so they won't dry out.

2. Take a board, and starting in the center, wrap your first coil around itself in a flat spiral. This will be the bottom of the bowl. As you place the coil use your fingers to work the clay into a continuous mass. Leave no gaps or cracks. Each strip of clay must be firmly attached to the adjoining piece.

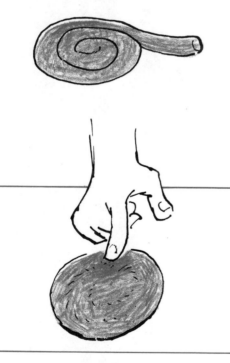

3. When the base of your bowl is as wide as you want it, turn it upside down and make sure the other side is firmly joined together. Then turn it back again.

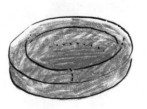

4. Now you can start building up the sides. Lay down a coil along the edge of your base and weld it into place by pressing and smoothing with your fingers or modeling tool. Do this on the inside as well as the outside. When you've made a complete circle cut off the excess and join the ends.

5. When the first coil of the wall is on, start with the second. Do the same thing—smoothing and pressing as you go. Make sure the joint where the ends of the coil meet is not directly on top of the first joint.

6. In order to get a curve in your bowl, you will have to vary the size of the circles. If they keep getting larger, the bowl will spread out. To make a bowl with a bulge in the middle, you would have to start with small circles, let them get larger, then gradually smaller again.

7. Finish off your bowl by working over the outside to get a neat, consistent surface. If you want to add any decoration, now is the time to do it. Remember the first experimental tiles you made? Perhaps some of the decorative textures you used there would look nice on this bowl.

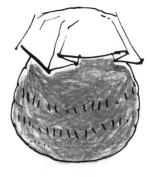

8. Finally, put it aside to dry. Make sure the top doesn't dry out before the bottom does. This is usually the case, and might cause cracks. It can be avoided by turning the bowl upside down, or by retarding the drying at the top by means of damp rags. When the bowl is thoroughly dry, fire it. If you intend to put liquids in the bowl, it should be glazed on the inside. The glaze will prevent the liquid from seeping into the walls of the bowl. (See page 58 for information about glazing.)

LAUGHING HEAD, *Vera Cruz*
American Museum of
Natural History

HEAD, *Greek*
Metropolitan Museum of Art

HEAD, *Nayarit style, Mexico*
American Museum of Natural History

Using Clay Coils To Make A Head

All materials impose their limitations. For example, if you were using a thick, large brush to make a drawing, you couldn't very well make fine lines or delicate details. And similarly, if you are working with clay, you can't make thin fingers or long, fragile eyelashes. The clay limits you to dense, compact shapes. It is a strong material in this form, but is delicate and breakable when its limitations are ignored.

The heads illustrated on the opposite page are all compact and quite simple. There are no thin ears, no narrow necks, no delicate projections. Forms of this sort have a way of falling off as the clay dries or is fired. In these heads the emphasis is on simple basic shapes. The head at the top of the page is a beautiful thing because

33

of the broad flat planes, the bold silhouette, the balance of one mass against another. In all these heads, the limitations of the clay have been respected.

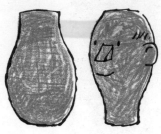

The shape of a human head is not very different from that of a vase. For example, look at the vase illustrated on the left. If you turned it upside down, and added a nose, eyes and ears, it would make a fine head. Here is how to build up a head with clay coils:

How To Make A Head With Clay Coils

1. Wedge up some clay and roll out a good supply of coils. They should be about 16 inches long and as thick as your thumb. Begin with the neck. Make it about two or three inches in diameter. The coils are built up and joined in exactly the same way you made the vase described in the previous section. Be sure each coil is firmly welded to the preceding one with no cracks, gaps or air pockets.

2. When the neck is an inch or two high, begin to make your coils lean outwards. This will start the shapes of the chin and back of the head.

3. Keep adding coils, bearing in mind the shapes you want. Let the coils bulge out a little where the mouth will go. Let them bulge *inwards* where the eyes will appear. And keep smoothing and welding the coils together—inside and outside—as you progress.

4. As the "walls" of the head get higher and higher they may begin to sag because of their increased weight. If this happens, brace it with a few pieces of wood, or put it aside for a few hours to dry a little and become firmer.

5. The nose is best made separately and added on with the use of slip.

6. Continue adding coils until you are almost to the top of the head. But don't close in the top yet. Leave enough room for your hand to reach inside to support the clay walls as you work on the smaller features.

7. Once you have the basic head shape, begin to refine the surface. Use a small block of wood and *gently* tap the clay while supporting it from inside with your hand. Now is the time to develop a neat surface and flowing contour.

8. Make the forehead a strong, round form. Get the curve of the cheeks, the line of the jaw. If you don't know how these forms look, examine someone's head, or look at yourself in a mirror.

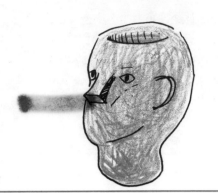

9. Make the ears from a separate slab of clay and attach them with slip. The eyes can be made in a variety of ways: a hole cut right through the clay, or a small clay ball added and then scooped out in the center. Or maybe you want to *draw* the eyes on the clay. On a separate piece of clay make a few experiments to see what can be done.

10. The expression of a head is largely determined by the shape of the mouth. If the corners are up, you have a smiling head; corners down— a frowning head. The mouth can be suggested by a simple line, or you can add two strips of clay for lips and model them. Perhaps you want to cut right through the clay wall and have an open mouth—singing or laughing.

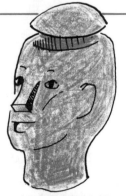

11. When you are finished with the features, cut out a "lid" from a slab of clay. Trim it to the exact size of the opening at the top of the head. Seal it in place with slip.

12. Finally, suggest the hair. A few decorative lines or variations in texture will do the trick. Don't try to put in every hair—it can't be done, and wouldn't look like much if it could be done. If you are making a girl's head, with lots of hair, you will have to add extra clay as shown. Allow the head to dry thoroughly. Then fire it.

There are, of course, other methods of making a head in addition to the coil method. A head can be modeled solid, then cut apart, hollowed out, and put together again with slip. You could also build up a head using slabs.

But what is most important in making a head is not the method you use, but the kind of forms and shapes and expression you get. If they are strong and vigorous, and the head has a well balanced, unfussy look, you will have a handsome object, regardless of which method you use.

HEAD OF A YOUTH WEARING AN
ASSYRIAN HELMET, *Cypriote,*
VII Century B.C.
Metropolitan Museum of Art
Color has been used on this
head to emphasize details
such as eyes and lips.

SEATED FIGURE, *Mexico*
American Museum of Natural History

SEATED FIGURE, *by Aristide Maillol*
Museum of Modern Art

SPOUTED POTTERY JAR, *Colima, Mexico*
American Museum of Natural History

FEMALE FIGURE, *Cypriote*
Metropolitan Museum of Art

SEATED FIGURE, *Mexico*
American Museum of Natural History

Figures In Clay

The human figure is one of the more difficult subjects for clay because the shapes of a human being are not the shapes that are best for clay. As you know, thin, long shapes in clay are not strong. And the human figure, with arms and legs and neck has many such forms. Therefore, when you make a figure in clay, you must do one of two things: You may choose to put the figure in a position where the forms are bunched up with a minimum of projections. (The statue on the preceding page is like this.) Or else you may *modify* the shape of the figure, giving it a thick neck, heavy arms and legs. You'll notice that all the figures shown here are quite compact. When an arm or leg does project, it is a very heavy arm or leg, or else—like the figure below and on the left with the missing right arm—it is broken off!

WOMAN BAKING CAKES IN AN OVEN,
Boeotian, VI Century B.C.
Metropolitan Museum of Art

STANDING FIGURE, *Mexico*
American Museum of Natural History

The Squish-Squash-Pull-Push-Poke Method

The figure illustrated at the top of this page is made by what I call the "squish-squash-push-pull-poke" method. This method is different from the ones described in the previous sections of this book, in that it is a good deal less planned and ordered. This is how it works:

1. Wedge up a piece of clay about as big as an orange. It should be somewhat on the soft side.

2. Pick up this lump of clay and begin to squish, squash, pull, push, and poke it. (Now you know how this method gets its name.)

3. Keep looking carefully at the shapes the clay gets into. Let the clay *tell you* what it wants to be!

4. Sooner or later you'll begin to see something that will suggest an idea. Perhaps a fold of clay will look like an arm or a leg. Or a squished-out piece somewhere will remind you of a head. You may see an animal or abstract design. Once you see something, control the clay and squish, poke and push it into the shapes you want.

5. Let's say you've discovered the suggestion of a figure—by rounding the clay in the center you can suggest the waist. A little squeeze below the head and you have the neck. Pinch the front of the head and you have a nose.

6. And you can, of course, make additional separate parts of the body and add them on. If you like, you can also place the figure on a seat and base made of clay slabs.

7. As the figure begins to emerge from the clay you will probably want to use a modeling tool for better control, and to remove any unwanted pieces of clay. If the clay is too soft to control properly, set it aside to dry for a few hours.

8. If your figure has any very large, dense masses, hollow them out by poking a pencil into them. Too massive a piece of clay will dry very slowly and won't fire well.

9. Finishing touches can be put on your piece when it has dried overnight and is leather-hard. Then let it dry completely and finally, fire it.

This method of working is very sculptural. The soft, responsive feeling of clay is retained. The finished piece will usually have the undulating, soft quality of your clay. Many artists feel that a work is successful only when the special quality of the material used is evident. The sculpture by Rodin reproduced in the margin manages to suggest the soft and responsive feel of the clay in which it was originally modeled.

MONUMENT TO BALZAC,
by Auguste Rodin
Museum of Modern Art

Making The Figure Out Of A Slab

Another way to make the figure is to start with a clay slab and cut out a "gingerbread" man. The fellow on the left and the angel illustrated at the top of the next page were made this way. A small angel makes a fine decoration for a Christmas tree, or you can simply hang it from

the ceiling by a thread. Angels like these look especially nice hung in groups of three or four. A little "cloud" of angels is a striking decoration in any room.

1. Wedge up some clay and roll it out into a slab. With a knife cut out the shape of the figure. Then cut out the shape of the wings.

2. Attach the wings to the body, using slip. Now you have the rough beginnings of your angel. Bend the wings until you get a graceful sweeping shape. If the wings won't stay in the position you give them, prop them up with little blocks of wood.

3. The body probably looks rather flat and uninteresting at this point, so add clay to give it roundness and form. Suggest the chest and stomach and thighs.

4. If the figure is too soft and sags when you pick it up and handle it, let it dry for a few hours. Then look at it from all sides. How does the back look? You will no doubt want to do a little modeling there, too. Try giving the figure some animation with a little twist or curve. You don't want your angel to look like a cut-out paper doll.

5. Do you want to add any decoration? A few lines to suggest the feathers in the wings, perhaps, or a pattern on the dress, or folds in the skirt. Finally, poke two holes in the wings so that you can attach strings. When it has dried you can fire it.

This angel is, of course, the simplest kind of figure. But you can work this way to start larger and more complex figures or groups of figures. But remember, if you work on a larger scale with heavy masses, the clay will have to be hollowed out. This is particularly true if the clay you are using has no grog in it.

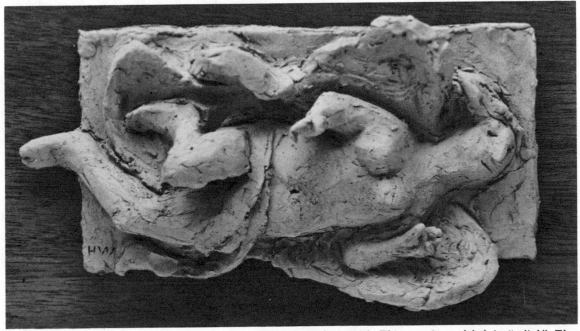

Here is another angel. This one is modeled in "relief." That means it is attached to, and grows out of a clay slab background.

Animals In Clay

Animals are great fun to make in clay. The variety of shapes and forms that animals come in provide endless possibilities for ceramic sculpture. Their vigorous, bold, massive forms make for handsome design.

If you think about the animals illustrated here, you'll realize that none of them is very realistic. They have all been simplified and adapted to the limitations of clay. Nevertheless, they all retain the character of the real animal. The hippopotamus, for example, has the heavy, clumsy quality of the real animal, even though it has a delicate flower glazed on its side. The owl has the sleepy, feathery feeling of a real owl. The same is true of the roly-poly pig. A pig like this is not very difficult to make. Here is how you do it:

OWL, *Contemporary Mexican*

GOAT, *Boeotian, VI Century B.C.*
Metropolitan Museum of Art

47

A Roly-Poly Pig

This pig is formed of two half balls of clay stuck together. Nose, ears, feet and tail are added onto the basic ball-shaped body to make the completed pig.

1. Wedge up some clay and roll it out into a slab.

2. Get a small light bulb and wrap it tightly with aluminum foil. This is to prevent the clay from sticking to the bulb. The bulb should be small—about 10-watt size. Otherwise you would end up with a rather large pig.

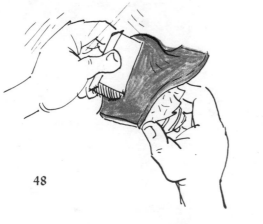

3. Cut a piece of clay slab about four inches square. Press it over the foil and the light bulb. Tap it with a block of wood to get the perfect half round shape of the bulb.

4. Cut around the clay at the widest part of the bulb and remove the excess. Then remove the clay along with the aluminum foil from the bulb. Now peel off the aluminum foil.

5. Put the foil around the bulb once more and repeat the entire process. You now have two half balls.

6. Roughen the edges, add slip and press the two halves together. This is the body. It is hollow, of course. Otherwise it would be hard to fire.

7. Go over the body with a small block of wood or modeling tool until you have a clean, round shape free of lumps and bumps.

8. Make four small clay cones for the legs and attach them with slip. The nose is a small cylinder attached in the same way.

9. The ears are made from a flattened-out piece of clay, bent into the shape you want. Don't make them too thin. The tail is simply a thin roll of clay twisted into a circle and stuck on where tails usually go.

If you want this pig to have a practical purpose, cut a little slit in his back. It's now a piggy bank. The only trouble with this kind of bank is that if the pig has turned out at all well, you will not want to destroy it—regardless of how badly you want to spend your savings! If you don't cut a slit for coins, you will have to punch a little hole in him somewhere to let out the expanded air during the firing process.

Now put him aside to dry. But keep little scraps of damp rags on the ears for a day or so. Otherwise they might dry out too fast and crack off. When completely dry, the pig can be fired.

Other Animals

The ball shape which makes the body of the pig can be made into a great many things besides a pig. The shape of a ball is so fundamental, its possibilities are limited only by your imagination. A number of things can be made from this starting point, as illustrated below, and no doubt you can think of many others yourself.

Small animals that don't have large, massive bodies can be made solid. You can build up your forms little by little, firmly squeezing the clay together. The alligator illustrated above was made this way. Notice the way the little stuck-on pellets of clay suggest the rough, scaly skin of this animal. (If there is no grog in your clay you should not attempt to fire anything thicker than about ¾ of an inch. With grog you can fire solids two or three inches thick.)

HORSE'S HEAD, *Chinese, Han Dynasty*
Metropolitan Museum of Art

DOVE ON A POMEGRANATE,
Lydian. Metropolitan Museum
of Art

DOG, *Colima, Mexico*
American Museum of Natural History

More Complex Projects

When a construction in clay gets beyond a certain size and complexity it begins to present various problems. It becomes difficult to keep one part from drying out faster than another and developing cracks. It is sometimes tricky to keep it from sagging. Also, many kilns are small and just don't have room for large pieces.

In order to avoid these difficulties, it is sometimes advisable to divide your piece into separate sections, and then fasten them together *after* they are fired. There are glues available which are so powerful it is a simple matter to bond separate parts permanently into a single, strong unit.

All the objects shown here are made of several separate sections. The Chinese lantern at the far left is made of five pieces cemented together with an epoxy cement. The bird bath in the next picture is also made of five pieces—four for the shape that holds the water, plus the base. The bird feeder above is strung together with thin fishing line.

A Chinese Lantern

The lantern, at first glance, may seem a rather large and complicated undertaking. But if you break it down into separate parts, you'll see that each section is just

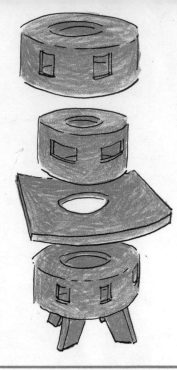

a little bowl with a top and bottom, and with windows cut in the sides.

The Chinese often carved these lanterns from stone and placed them in their gardens. But they look equally nice in clay, and make a very festive table decoration, especially if you put a lighted candle inside.

The Bird Bath

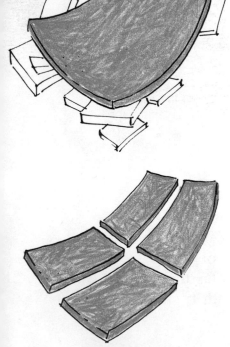

The bird bath shown on page 52 is made from one large, heavy slab of clay. The slab is gradually formed into a concave shape by raising and propping up the outside edges. Keep tapping down the center of the slab, and keep raising the props around the outside.

The clay is allowed to dry to a firm, leather-hard state, and then carefully cut into quarters. The base is made separately, and the whole thing cemented together with a strong, waterproof adhesive (such as an epoxy cement) after firing.

It is advisable to glaze the inside of the bath. (See page 58 for information about glazing.) Otherwise, the water would be absorbed into the clay.

The little rod structure that stands at one end of the bird bath is simply a few ⅛-inch dowels stuck into holes previously poked in the clay. The cross-pieces are fastened with tightly wrapped copper wire. This makes a little perch or "diving board" for the birds. They will sit up there and then splash in the water and have a marvelous time.

Combining Other Materials With Clay

Since thin, linear shapes cannot be made in clay, what can you do when your idea demands the use of shapes of this sort? You must either discard the idea, or use clay in *combination* with other suitable materials.

If, for example, you wanted to make a bird with long, thin legs, you could use clay for the body, then find some stiff wire or thin wood dowels for the legs. That's the way the bird up above was made. The holes for the legs to fit into were poked into the clay while soft. Then, after firing, the legs were fitted in place and the bird

This little gumdrop bird has tooth picks stuck into holes in the clay. This could also be used to serve olives or bits of cheese.

mounted on a little wood base. Metal rods and dowels lend themselves very nicely to use with clay because their thin shape is such a pleasant and dramatic contrast with the bulkiness of clay.

Clay Jewelry

Pins, necklaces and pendants can all be made of clay in many shapes and forms. Ceramic jewelry looks best when glazed. The plain fired clay with its natural color is a little too undramatic for jewelry. Colors — glossy blues, vivid reds, greens or yellows — make your jewelry exciting.

Clay lends itself to jewelry on the grand scale. Tiny beads or fingernail-sized pendants don't come out very well. Clay is too hard to handle when used very small. Work big! And pay particular attention to your glazing.

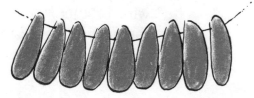

The clay used for jewelry should, if possible, be of a fine texture. There are special white jewelry clays available from ceramic supply stores. If you don't have any of this, you can of course, use any clay you happen to have.

Beads for a necklace are made by rolling out a long "snake" of clay and then cutting it up into even pieces. The pieces are rolled between your palms until round, then holed by means of a thin nail. When the beads are dry and you glaze them, be careful to keep the glaze from running into the hole and clogging it. Page 60 describes the method used for firing glazed beads.

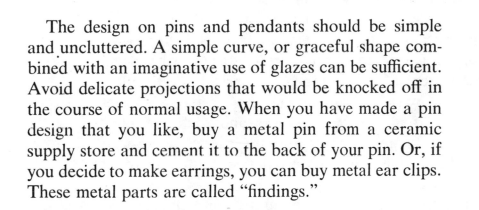

BEADS, *Egyptian,*
XI Dynasty
Metropolitan Museum of Art

The design on pins and pendants should be simple and uncluttered. A simple curve, or graceful shape combined with an imaginative use of glazes can be sufficient. Avoid delicate projections that would be knocked off in the course of normal usage. When you have made a pin design that you like, buy a metal pin from a ceramic supply store and cement it to the back of your pin. Or, if you decide to make earrings, you can buy metal ear clips. These metal parts are called "findings."

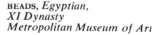

Glazing, Firing And Using The Potter's Wheel

The next six pages of this book describe some of the more technical matters involved in finishing and firing clay. Even if you don't intend to do your own firing, or plan to do any glazing, read this section. It will round out your understanding of the ceramic art.

Glazes

A glaze is a coating which is painted on the surface of a finished clay piece. The glaze is composed of various minerals mixed with water. When subjected to the high temperatures of the kiln, the minerals melt and fuse to form a very hard, permanent coating over the clay. The bowls and vases illustrated at the top of the opposite page have a glazed surface.

Glazes are usually applied with a brush, though large commercial potteries sometimes spray the glaze on, or the clay piece is dipped into a container of glaze.

Glazes are used for two reasons. The first is to provide pottery with a smooth, non-porous surface which will prevent water or food from being absorbed into the clay. The second reason glazes are used is aesthetic. Glazes come in a great variety of colors and surfaces. They enable you to give variety and decorative interest to clay surfaces that might otherwise be a little plain or uninteresting.

Designs and patterns can be painted onto clay, almost as you would paint with paints on paper. The one big difference, however, is that the glaze colors are very mild and pale looking when applied. It is only after the firing that the real, intense colors appear.

It is possible to make your own glazes by grinding certain minerals into a fine powder and mixing them with water. But the beginner will get better results, and save a great deal of time, if he uses the prepared liquid glazes which are sold at all ceramic supply stores.

*Egyptian,
Metropolitan Museum of Art*

Glazing can be an extremely complicated part of ceramics if gone into thoroughly. If you want to prepare your own glazes and understand what makes them perform as they do, you will have to study some of the textbooks which give formulas and procedures and other detailed information.

For the beginner, there is one sure way of getting acquainted with glazes quickly—by experimenting. Make two or three dozen small tiles, dry them, and try different glazes and different combinations of glazes on them. See what happens when you paint one glaze color over another. Put on the glaze heavily or sparingly, in dots or in stripes. If it will fit, dip a tile into a jar of glaze. Use a small brush to paint some kind of design onto a tile. When all these different experiments have been fired you will have a sample reference of glaze possibilities. Then you can proceed to glaze a larger piece with some idea of what the final result will be.

Other Decorative Techniques

Another way to decorate the surface of a clay piece is by means of slip. If you use a different color clay and make a slip mixture, this can be painted onto your clay and will show up quite vividly. Be sure your base clay and the slip clay are quite different in value. A white clay over a terra cotta, for example, would work well. The striped horse shown on page 47 was decorated in this way.

A variation of the above method is called "sgraffito." Clay of one color is completely painted over with a slip of another color. Then, with a sharp tool, lines and patterns are scratched through the top layer, exposing the clay underneath.

Stacking The Kiln

The kiln which is used for firing clay usually reaches a temperature of about 2000 degrees Fahrenheit. A kitchen oven gets no hotter than 550 degrees, so it cannot be used for firing clay.

Clay changes from its normal plastic state into a very hard, dense material when subjected to these high temperatures. It can no longer be softened with water, as plain, unfired clay can. The plates, cups and saucers you eat and drink from are made of clay that has been glazed and fired.

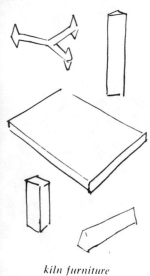

kiln furniture

The process of placing clay to be fired into a kiln is called "stacking." It should be done with a great deal of care and thought so that you can fit in the greatest number of pieces. When no glazes are used, it is possible to let the different pieces touch one another. One piece can rest on top of another. You can even put one piece inside another, in the case of different sized bowls. But at no time should anything touch the sides of the kiln. Kiln "furniture" of the kind illustrated in the margin is used to help make a place for everything.

If you are firing clay that has been glazed, you must keep the pieces from touching one another. If you didn't, the glaze would run off onto adjoining pieces, causing them to stick together and making a general mess.

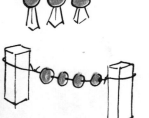

Beads which have been glazed must be strung on a high temperature steel or nichrome wire which is suspended between two props. An alternative method is to place each bead on a little "pyramid." The drawings in the margin show how this is done.

The Firing

When the kiln is properly stacked, the lid or door is closed—but not completely. A little piece of wood or clay is propped under the door to keep it slightly open. Let us assume that this is an electric kiln, because most small kilns are electric. It will probably have a switch for *low, medium,* and *high* temperatures.

With the door open slightly the switch is turned on to *low*. After an hour the door is closed, and after about another hour the switch is turned to *medium*.

As you see, the temperature in a kiln must be increased *very gradually*. An abrupt increase in temperature would shatter the pieces inside the kiln. In about one more hour the switch can be turned to *high*. A small kiln will probably have reached firing temperature after about two hours at *high*. But this time will vary greatly, depending on the size and type of kiln you are using. A very large kiln might take several days to reach the proper temperature, and a very small jewelry kiln might do the trick in an hour.

Kilns are fired by means of gas and oil, as well as electricity. But kilns using these fuels are usually quite large and used only by experienced, professional ceramists.

Temperatures

How hot should the kiln get? It must reach the firing temperature. This is the temperature at which the clay changes from a fragile material which can be dissolved in water, into a hard and durable material which is unaffected by moisture. This temperature will vary with the clay you are using. Some clays need more heat than others. The average terra cotta clay, of the sort recommended in this book, should be fired to approximately 1800 degrees. This amount of heat is suitable for most of the clays commonly used. Though some china and porcelain clays need temperatures up to around 2600 degrees.

If you want to be sure, you can determine the best temperatures for the clay you are using by firing some experimental clay samples to various temperatures and then comparing them to see which is strongest.

Another factor that will decide the amount of heat needed is your glaze—if you are using glazes. You'll find that the commercial glazes which are sold by ceramic supply stores indicate on the label what temperatures are recommended. If the temperature recommended for the glaze is much *less* than that required for the clay, you will have to fire twice—once for the clay—then once again after the glaze has been applied to the fired clay.

After the kiln has reached the firing temperature turn it off and forget about it until the next morning. The kiln must not be opened until it is almost cool. If you open a kiln when it is very hot the cooler air in the room will crack the kiln and everything in it.

How can you tell what the temperature inside the kiln is? Some larger kilns have built-in thermometers. (They are called "pyrometers.") You can read the dial and know instantly what the temperature is inside the kiln.

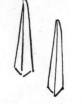

pyrometric cones

cone has sagged

Other kilns have peepholes that you can look through to observe "pyrometric cones." Pyrometric cones are made of a special material which sags at specific temperatures. They are placed inside the kiln, in view of the peephole. If, for example, you want your kiln to go to 1900 degrees, you can place a cone which will sag at about that temperature into the kiln (cone 04). When you peep in and see that the cone is beginning to sag, you know that the kiln has reached this temperature. It is time to turn off the kiln. Pyrometric cones are numbered to correspond to different temperatures. A few of the more commonly used cones and the temperatures at which they will sag are shown below:

cone number	degrees Fahrenheit	cone number	degrees Fahrenheit
012	1544	04	1922
010	1634	02	2003
08	1733	1	2057
06	1841	2	2075

As you can see, the proper use of a kiln is a little tricky. *Do not* attempt to use anything but a small electric kiln unless you have somebody with experience to supervise what you are doing.

The Potter's Wheel

The potter's wheel is a basic tool in the making of vases, bowls, pots, or any round, symmetrical clay object. Basically it is a small, round table which revolves—much like a phonograph turntable. Some potter's wheels are turned by an electric motor; others are turned by a foot pedal.

A plaster "bat," or base, is placed on the wheel, and the clay is centered on this. As the wheel revolves the clay is shaped and controlled as shown in the drawings below. If you are fortunate enough to have access to a potter's wheel, an entirely new realm of possibilities is open to you. You will need a great deal of practice and experience, however, before you'll be able to control the revolving clay with confidence, and some expert supervision is advisable.

bat centered on wheel and clay centered on bat

bat anchored to wheel with soft clay

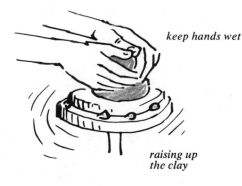

keep hands wet

raising up the clay

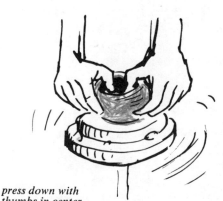

press down with thumbs in center to open up clay

This book has explained the basic techniques of ceramics. It has shown you the tremendous variety of shapes and forms that can be made with clay. But in order for you to keep learning and improving it is important that you see what other people have done and are doing. Look at the ceramics that are to be found in most museums. Look at the old Chinese and Japanese work and the work being produced by modern ceramists. What you produce — in ceramics, or any other medium — is a result of looking and examining and thinking about everything related to what you are trying to do.

Explanation of Terms

CERAMICS: the technique of fashioning clay into a permanent, fired object of practical or artistic value.

FIRING: the process of heating clay to a very high temperature, at which time it changes into a hard and durable material.

GLAZE: a thin, surface coating which is baked onto clay to make the clay impervious to water, or to decorate it. It is available in many colors.

GROG: clay that has been fired and then ground up into small particles. It is added to clay to decrease shrinkage, cracking and warping.

KILN: the furnace in which clay is fired.

LEATHER-HARD: refers to clay which is partially dry.

SLIP: clay mixed with water to make a soupy consistency. It is used for sticking parts together.

THROWING: the art of forming clay while it is revolving on a potter's wheel.

WEDGING: the process of cutting clay apart and then slamming it together again to remove air pockets and get a uniform consistency.

Thanks and acknowledgments are due the following organizations and individuals for their cooperation and generous help in the preparation of this book: the Metropolitan Museum of Art, New York; the Museum of Modern Art, New York; the American Museum of Natural History, New York; Mr. Albert Jacobson; and Jane and Tauno Kauppi.

The ceramic work and illustrations are by the author unless otherwise credited.